1

God-IN-Cidences

No Coincidences

Pat Watson

Dedication

This book is dedicated to my wonderful husband Tom and five children: Kim, Kelly, Kyle, Tommy and Zach. My journey of life has been so meaningful and rich because you have traveled along side of me. My hope is that these stories will enrich you and your posterity down through the generations.

Prologue

"In his heart a man plans his course, but the Lord determines his steps."

Proverbs 16:9

It's March 17, 2019, and I'm writing these memoirs while sitting in the lower level of the Basilica of San Francesco d'Assisi near the crypt of this holy saint. When I discovered my dream was going to materialize with this week in Italy, I felt a strong desire to write about this experience and others that have completely astonished me. I call them God-IN-cidences because they are so remarkable that only our Divine Creator could have orchestrated their occurrences. And the ones I relate are only the ones I was keen enough to recognize!

I believe God-IN-cidences occur right in front of us all the time, but we are so busy scrambling to get things done and perform our own agenda that we don't recognize them. They are like love taps on our shoulders but so gentle that we need to be ready and alert for them. Charging to work, raising busy families, sports, activities, technologies, and a constant barrage of noise prevent us from being sensitive to the Spirit's workings.

The few divine touches I'm going to share with you, that I've recognized, make me long even more for the ones I've missed. I'm sure there were aha-reverent moments that passed me by while I was teaching and raising five children.

My wish is that this sharing will cause you to open your spiritual eyes and be looking for your God-IN-cidences. They are true blessings and joys in this journey of life.

Table of Contents

God-IN-cidence #1 Vacation Surprises

"Trust in the Lord with all your heart and lean not on your own understanding; in all your ways acknowledge him, and he will make your paths straight."

Proverbs 3:5

March 17th, a day most people recognize as St. Patrick's Day, and I certainly do because my name is Patricia Ann Watson. Did I plan to start this book in Italy on the feast day of my patron saint? No way. I was in such a hurry to get ready for this trip that it didn't occur to me until I looked at my cell phone today that it was the 17th of March, kind of a nice little surprise for me.

I will relate various short stories of God-IN-cidences during my lifetime, but the most recent one is how I'm in Assisi now.

I grew up in a small farming community near the Mississippi River by St. Louis, Missouri. The population was near 500 residents when I was young. I had a simple and happy childhood as the oldest of five other siblings. My parents raised us to love God, work hard, and do the right thing. I would ride my bike a couple miles to church in the summertime to the parish of St. Francis. Since I attended the grade school next to it, I heard of St. Francis and his life's mission many times.

I met a wonderful man in college who was going to be an Air Force pilot after graduation. Tom and I married in 1970. Since he became a commercial pilot after his service commitment was finished, we've enjoyed free, stand-by travel all over the world. We had been to Rome and other Italian cities but never to Assisi.

Last year I tried to book a week in Assisi during my spring break from college teaching. Since our time share company only had one property in that vicinity, it was already full the week we needed it by the time I checked. We enjoyed a wonderful vacation instead in one of their properties in Scotland, part of the heritage of my husband. This year I started five months ahead of time looking online. Much to my delight they had one, and only one unit available, and it was for this 3rd week of March, my spring break week! I was so excited that I booked it immediately before it was gone.

Now, you may be thinking that's just random luck and no big deal, but I don't see it that way. Then I especially didn't when three weeks later, a friend of mine who rents a house near us every February texted this strange request, "Pat, do you mind if we have a shipment of wines, cheese and pasta from ASSISI, ITALY sent to your house in Florida because it will probably arrive there before we rent our house in February?" I didn't even bother to text her back. I picked up the phone and said, "What was that again?" She explained that a travel agent friend of hers recommended this family from Assisi who travel for a couple months in the winter to various places in the United States. They host dinners and wine sampling in hopes people will enjoy and order from them. My friend had never met them but decided it would be fun.

I was ecstatic! It was an "Aha, thank you God" moment for me right then and there. It also sealed the deal for me. I knew I WANTED to go to Assisi, but now I knew there was a reason even bigger than my desire. I didn't know exactly why I was supposed to visit there, but I knew it was God appointed with these two happenings lining up. I call these God-IN-cidences.

It was then I felt a strong compelling to put these incidents in print along with others that I have experienced. Why? Because so many people are wandering around this planet, thinking there's no plan, no guidance, no reason other than to survive and find a little pleasure along the way. I'm hoping that sharing these stories will open peoples' eyes to look for God-taps in their lives. He loves each one of us equally and with a burning Love that we can't even imagine. These God-IN-cidences shake up our melancholy and the stupor in which we trudge. They get our attention so we MUST at least acknowledge that a Divine Presence has just entered our little space.

We were invited to the Italian feast at Kay and Ed's, and it was fabulous. I had never eaten truffles before or sampled wines as expensive as the ones the Italians served us. We thoroughly enjoyed ourselves and were delighted to tell our hosts that we were scheduled to go to Assisi three weeks later and would visit their shop then. They were happy to hear that news also.

Today was the day we visited their shop, March 17. We finished enjoying a delicious lunch at their shop after celebrating Mass above the crypt of St. Francis. I went back to the crypt and sat in the last pew to begin this book. To God be the glory.

God-IN-cidence #2 Assisi Arrival and Highlights

"Delight yourself in the Lord and he will give you the desires of your heart."

Psalm 37:4

Since I was aware of the two God-IN-cidences He gave us about this trip, I had peace during the craziness of trying to non-rev (free stand-by traveling for airline employees) across the ocean. The night before our trip, the 737 Max plane from Orlando to Miami was cancelled and grounded due to faulty mechanical problems, so we had to drive. First glitch in our plans.

When traffic slowed on the turnpike, don't stress I thought because I knew we were destined to be in Assisi. Then, when I took an express lane to hasten our trip, and it ended up veering in a large semi-circle around the city, thus lengthening our miles, Tom was rather upset. Don't worry dear, we are going to make it in time. No problem....God has the plan.

When we got to the airport and tried to check in, the AIRITALIA agent said there is no record of us on his passenger list. We were astounded! Tom said there must be a mistake because his former airline's agent said we were listed on the flight. The agent looked again, said we weren't on it and it was too LATE to put us on it. I smiled and said, "Please try." He said, "Give me your passports just in case and come back in 45 minutes. We'll see what is happening then." No problem....God has the plan.

Now, since I arranged this trip and was more in tune with the two unique blessings to get it, I was not ruffled, but my dear husband was having a hard time. Pilots are used to every dial and switch in the cockpit being in exactly the right position, and he likes his affairs that way also. He looked like he had just walked into a disaster by then. I said, "Let's go get something to eat while we wait and try not to worry." We did, and then went back at exactly 45 minutes later. The agent said that the flight was full but hurry on down to the gate just in case. No problem....God has the plan.

We half ran to the gate, and there were two other people standing there. That agent calls their names, and they go down the jetway. The next minute he looks at us and asks why we are there. We say we are standing by for that flight. He checked our names on his computer and said, "HURRY-GO" and closed the jet way door behind us. This time we did run and got possibly the last seats on the plane. We didn't have time to look around because we had to sit, strap in and get ready for takeoff. Gratia Dios! Italy here we come!!

Today I'm writing on March 19, 2019, the feast of St. Joseph. Again, I go back to the crypt and sit in the back to gather my thoughts. So many reverent pilgrims pass by me to walk up front around the remains of this holy saint, a man who communed so closely with the Father that he blessed him with the stigmata, the sacred wounds of Jesus. Francis showed the world he lived in how to be at peace with nature and all people. He renounced all worldly wealth that he would have inherited from his wealthy father and chose to minister to the poor instead. I don't know what is was like in the 12th century, but I felt a tangible peace as I walked the streets of Assisi. PAX...how our world yearns for it. PAX

March 20th was our last day to walk the streets and explore. Tom and I stopped at a coffee shop for a cappuccino after touring the castle of Rocco Maggiore. A friendly American man just 'happened' to drop in for a coffee at the same time. After exchanging greetings, he asked how long of a stay we had. We said we leave the next day at a very early hour. Then, he said his wife and he had been coming to visit Assisi for 14 years, and six months ago they moved there permanently. He asked if we had seen various sites such as the Hermitage and we said no. He told us to follow him to his house a short distance away, and he would write out a list for us to see.

As we passed by an abandoned church, he said we needed to go in. It was the Guido Deltoni della Grazia. It was now used as a religious art museum. A very large Tau cross had the slight outline of Jesus carved into it. Beautiful Madonnas carved from many wood types were encased in separate cylindrical glasses in a circle. I purchased one because the artist had sculpted it so that when turned, it showed four different positions and roles of Mary. These were marvelous images of her life, such as carrying a water jug, being pregnant with the Messiah, kneeling in prayer and holding the infant Jesus. It also fit in the curve of your right hand and was so comforting. This stop was one of the highlights of our trip, and we would have never discovered it on our own.

He then took us to his newly purchased, but very old, stone house and gave us a list of "must-sees" that day. We followed his advice and were delighted with his choices. Tom agreed with me that this was NO coincidence that we just happened to pick the same coffee shop as an American who knew the city like the back of his hand. What a gift. God's plan again. Oh, blessed God-IN-cidences.

March 21st, as we opened our wooden arched window covers, we stared at the hills of Umbria. It was hard to leave this place of peace and tranquility. I prayed God imprinted on our memories the specialness of this place as we continued our journey home.

As I was packing the last remaining items, I remembered I purchased two rounds of specialty cheeses from our Italian friends' shop. I was hoping they wouldn't spoil on the long trip home since we had a day lay-over in Spain. I was still thinking about that when I opened a front zippered compartment of my suitcase and inside was a red shoe of mine that I had been missing. Yeh. Then I reached way down to the bottom, and there was an insulated rectangular carrying case for hot/cold items with two cold packs. Thank you, God. I had forgotten to unpack that compartment when I brought it back to Florida from our apartment in Missouri. Perfect solution for getting my cheese back to the states without the chance of spoiling. So many surprises these few days.

So many delights. So many revelations of our Father's love. May our hearts be always open and expectant for the Father's gifts.

Taking back the rental car and waiting for a stand-by flight was smooth and easy this time. We even were given first class seats which rarely happens. As I lay prone, I reflected over the wonderful time we had and how I saw God's handprint on our time overseas.

God-IN-cidence #3 A Pointed Finger

"For this reason, a man will leave his father and mother and be united to his wife, and they will become one flesh."

Genesis 2:24

On September 18, 1967 as I walked into the gymnasium of my college for my first college dance, I saw a long arm stretched over the top of a couple girls' heads with an index finger of his hand pointed at me. I thought how strange but turned to look as the guy mouthed, "Want to dance?" I was a little taken aback at this unusual approach but noticed that he was very tall and cute. I had just begun attending that all-women's college that month. For their first mixer (dance), local men's colleges were invited. The ratio of men to women was about 5:1.

We danced and danced. Then we talked and shared our life stories. He had grown up in Saudi Arabia because his stepdad worked for Aramco oil company. He had gone to high school at Notre Dame in Rome and had traveled extensively. I was spell-bound because I grew up on a farm in a small town, and we only took vacations to the Ozarks, which was about 250 miles away. He then told me how he knew exactly what he wanted to do with his life: fly in the Air Force, move on to commercial flying, have a family, and travel. I loved adventures! As a child, I read every book I could get my hands on and lived vicariously.

Well, forty-nine years of marriage between us now, Tom and I have raised five wonderful children and have traveled the world.

I became a math teacher, and he has logged over 26,000 hours flying people to their destinations. We both enjoyed our careers and all our experiences. We've had a blessed life, and we realize it. Many joys, some heartaches, a few trials have happened over the years, but we feel so blessed.

Are you wondering what if his finger had pointed to a different girl? Was it fate, chance or God that made him single me out? Believe me, there certainly were prettier gals than me crammed in that gym. We were two people from opposite parts of the world with only our dreams and our faith in common. We would have never met or married if not for that split-second decision on Tom's part to point at me.

Can a person live with and love someone else other than their chosen mate? Yes, I believe so, but I believe our two lives were God-ordained to meet. When one marries, it encompasses more than the two individuals; it melds two extended families. All those connections are influenced by the union. Many people would call it fate or chance. I don't think so.

God-IN-cidence #4 Airplane Miracle

"Ask and it will be given to you; seek and you shall find; knock and the door will be opened to you. For everyone who asks receives; he who seeks finds; and to him who knocks, the door will be opened."

Matthew 7:7

This passage came alive for me the day our small airplane sold. We had committed to a four-way partnership when stationed in Montana. The plane provided trips home to the St. Louis area as well as to various other places. The pleasure of owning a plane was short-lived because it soon needed repairs and other expensive maintenance.

Then Tom decided to get out of the service and took a job flying for Ozark Airlines. I was thrilled. Finally, after six years of different bases while in the Air Force, I would be going back home because St. Louis was its headquarters. Since Tom was leaving the area and was the only experienced pilot, the other partners decided to sell the plane also.

This sounds like a simple solution to us moving and the partnership, but it wasn't. One of the partners was a doctor who had just opened his first restaurant. It went under shortly after he started it. He had lost a lot of money and desperately wanted his share of the plane's investment immediately. He would call us in St. Louis and demand we give him his money. The problem was we didn't have an extra dime. His harassing phone calls became a real nightmare for me because he threatened legal action. Another partner got laid off from his construction job, and a few weeks later the third partner lost his job also. What is going on I thought? Then, to compound the problem, Tom gets furloughed from Ozark Airlines. So, four men who had invested in a small airplane were unemployed, and none could afford the payments and maintenance fees.

I was teaching, and our daughter Kim was four and daughter Kelly was two. Tom was watching them to save daycare costs. We were scrimping on everything. We didn't want to take a huge loss on the plane and undersell it because everyone needed their share of the money.

I began praying as hard as I knew how at 29 years old, begging God to intervene. One day, while praying about it, I got this idea to ask God to have it sold for a fair price by a certain day. I had never asked God to do something on my schedule before, but we were desperate. February 1st was the date that popped into my mind, and so every day I asked Him to have a buyer call before February first. I even told the Christian teacher across the hall from me this is how I was praying. He thought that was the wrong way, I know. He smiled politely but didn't comment. I really believed God was going to rescue us by that date.

We had been advertising the plane in various newspapers and magazines for many months with no responses. I can still picture in my mind where I was in our bedroom when the phone rang with a potential buyer. It was JANUARY 30th about eight o'clock at night. I answered the phone, and a man asked if we had a Mooney airplane to sell. I said yes and ran to get Tom. He said he was in New Mexico; and after a few questions, he said he wanted to buy it! Tom said he would leave then and fly all night to get it to him.

When he arrived at the designated airport, the buyer met him with a cashier's check for the amount we advertised. No bargaining or even a test flight happened. Tom flagged a ride to the main airport and came home. We were ecstatic!

I went shouting and praising the Lord all through the house. I picked up Kim and Kelly and twirled them around dancing with joy. I'm sure King David felt more jubilation when he danced before the Lord, but it was a total release of sheer exaltation for me. I couldn't believe how good God was! He had rescued us.

I had a cake made from a bakery that said, "Praise the Lord." I took it to work and shared it and this story with my co-workers. I wanted everyone to know what God had done for us.

Forty years have passed since then and never has a date popped into my head like that when I've been praying. Most of the time I sense God telling me to trust His timing and to ask that His Will be done, not mine. Yet, in Matthew 9:29, it says, "According to your faith will it be done to you." God made it known to me then that He longs to bless us and give us good gifts.

We need to remember that when two blind men were shouting at Jesus, He said, "What do you want me to do for you?" Matthew 20:32

What do you want?

God-IN-cidence #5 Two Strangers Sent to Help Me

"Do not forget to show hospitality to strangers, for by so doing some people have shown hospitality to angels without knowing it."

Hebrews 13:2

It was a beautiful day, August 26, 2015, in St. Peters, Missouri, and I decided when I awoke to ride my bike to church that day. Tom and I had purchased a new home in January of that year and moved our furniture in but then left the next day to spend the winter in our Florida home. We had just returned in May after I finished my Florida teaching that spring semester. The home and area still felt brand new to us. I took my usual route through the park adjoining our subdivision to church. It had bike trails and was mostly on level terrain.

After Mass, I decided since it was such a gorgeous day, that Tom and I should get a tee time and play golf. He had just begun to teach me that winter in Florida, and I wanted to practice. Instead of my usual route, I decided to go a more direct route which meant I'd maneuver up and down over hills on a sidewalk next to a busy street. It was more arduous to navigate but more direct to our home.

As I rounded the top of a slight hill, I noticed something odd down at the bottom of it. I had never seen anything quite like it. As I approached, my thought was I hope I can steer past this hole. I now know it is called a storm sewage drain which is a semi-circle cut-out in the otherwise uniform width sidewalk. I didn't make it past. I awoke in an ambulance not even remembering my correct address. I had extensive bleeding from the nose, mouth and ear and deep abrasions above the eye.

I could call them angels, but they weren't. They were two real people that just "happened" to be driving on the street at exactly at the same time as crash. One was an off-duty fire chief that noticed the storm sewage drain when he drove past it and saw me rounding the hill. He said he thought I hope that woman sees that hazard. He slowed his car and was watching me out of his rearview mirror to see if I safely made it past. When I didn't, he halted traffic and called the ambulance. He said he found me twisted in my bike on the street. Then a RN stopped next, and she supported my neck while he untangled me. They waited for the ambulance together.

I was told all this much later. Two "angel-like" trained medical people sent to drive on Ohmes Road at 9:15 a.m. exactly when I needed them was my God-IN-cidence that day! I do believe real angels buffered my fall so that it wasn't debilitating or fatal.

I have two scars over my right eyebrow which remind me of God's deliverance that day. Though my face swelled, turned black and blue, and I had vertigo and dizziness for months, I now have no permanent injuries. Since I was not wearing a helmet (which I do now), I feel very blessed. When I met the fireman, who helped me that day, he said, "I thought you would be dead." No, God isn't finished with me yet. I get to write this book and tell of God's goodness.

God-IN-cidence #6 Home in a Diesel Pusher

"The Lord helps them and delivers them."

Psalm 37:40

Since my husband lived out of a suitcase his whole career, he was tired of packing and unpacking. We both love to travel so he decided a home on wheels was the way to go. He had been talking about this dream of his for years. I wasn't that thrilled, but I didn't want to squelch his enthusiasm about living in 300 square feet.

Off we went to look at RVs. They are amazing with all the luxuries crammed into such a small place with even slide outs to enlarge the rooms. I was impressed but still leery. He likes TV, and I like quiet reading time. How do you manage that on a rainy day? I prayed about it and felt led to let Tom, who spent so much of his time away from his family working so hard, have his dream. I decided I would learn to adjust.

We custom ordered a new one exactly with all the appointments we liked. He had to put $5000 down, but we did get the salesman to agree to a VERBAL agreement that if we had difficulty selling our house or if an emergency came up, we could back out of the deal. I kept praying for God's will, not mine, be done because I was getting more and more anxious about living in such cramped quarters.

One day Tom woke up and said, "If we decide to sell the RV in a couple years, we will lose a lot of equity. I don't think it's a good investment, so we shouldn't do it." Wow, what a surprise that was to me after hearing about his RV dream of traveling the states for years. I admitted I was getting more apprehensive about it also.

I figured we had lost the $5000 because we custom ordered it, yet we asked for our $5000 back. The salesman did honor his word and returned our money even though we had signed papers. We then bought our current home in Florida in a retirement area. We both love it and are so glad we are here. I believe it was a God-IN-cidence that we were given one of the many salesmen at that huge center who would honor his word over a written contract. How many people do that anymore? Thank you, God.

God-IN-cidence #7 God in a Thrift Store

"The Lord himself goes before you and will be with you; he will never leave you nor forsake you."

Deuteronomy 31:8

Since I crave the outdoors and because of the great weather in central Florida, I suggested to Tom that we have an outdoor tiled patio laid behind our lanai. He agreed it would be a nice addition to our place. I'm sitting there now on my recently purchased patio furniture writing this next God-IN-cidence.

Yesterday, I asked my neighbor if she wanted to go to our parish's re-sell it store shopping with me. It's full of donations from the community, and all proceeds go to the local Food Pantry. It's a great win-win for everybody. A lot of retirees bring way too many furnishings when they move to a smaller house and then are thrilled when volunteers from re-sell it stores will come take their donations away.

Looking for bargains and treasures at these shops is one of my latest hobbies. Since my neighbor had never been to one, I decided to show her two that were very close to us.

The first blessing occurred when I pulled into the parking lot and before us was a patio set displayed for sale. The oval table was surrounded with six beautiful fern green cushioned chairs which looked like new. That's here exactly for me I thought! I went in, paid, and planned for delivery. We walked around inside the store, but neither of us found anything else that we couldn't live without.

So, I told my neighbor I'd show her a bigger and better re-sell-it store down a couple blocks. The most amazing thing happened when we walked into that store. A volunteer worker walks right up to me and excitedly says, "You must see this murphy bed that just arrived. It's only been used once and is beautiful!" She went on and on, so I followed her to the back of the store.

I had no intention of spending $750 for a bed, but it was the perfect size for our study. It was light gray which is the color scheme of the study, and we were expecting a lot of guests in the next couple months! It folded up to look like a chest and had a large pull-out drawer at the bottom for storage. It was just perfect for my house. Tom was a little taken aback when I told him about my two purchases; but when I found the same murphy bed on Amazon for double the price, he was okay.

As we were driving home, Barb, my neighbor said, "That was amazing how that lady walked right up to you to tell you about the murphy bed since the store was full of other shoppers." No, not amazing at all----a God-IN-cidence. Thank you, God.

God-IN-cidence #8 Not Just an Ordinary Dream

"In the last days, God says, 'I will pour out my Spirit on all people, your sons and daughters will prophesy, your young men will see visions, your old men will dream dreams. Even on my servants, both men and women, I will pour out my Spirit in those days, and they will prophesy."

Acts 2:17-18

Under the Old Testament covenant, God poured out His Spirit on only chosen, special people. They were his prophets and priests. When Jesus died for us, ascended to heaven, and the Holy Spirit fell on the disciples, a new era began for believers. The Holy Spirit dwells in all believers and can move powerfully in modern day lives.

"If you then, though you are evil, know how to give good gifts to your children, how much more will your Father in heaven give the Holy Spirit to those who ask him?" Luke 11:13

Most of us receive fillings of the Holy Spirit at our baptism and confirmation. There are deeper levels of fillings if one seeks and asks. The Holy Spirit is a gentleman; he will not force himself on anyone who doesn't desire His presence.

I believe a lot of our dreams are just unconscious thoughts being brought to the surface of our minds when we sleep. Yet, some dreams are divine interventions in our lives like the many times revealed in Scripture. Joseph in the Old Testament was told in a dream that his brothers would bow down to him. After many trials and years, the dream manifested itself when his brothers bowed before him in Egypt.

In the New Testament, Joseph was told to take Mary as his wife after he found out she was pregnant by the Holy Spirit. "Joseph, son of David, do not be afraid to take Mary home as your wife, because what is conceived in her is from the Holy Spirit. She will give birth to a son, and you are to give him the name Jesus because he will save his people from their sins." Matthew 1: 20-21

God spoke to Samuel, Daniel and many others in dreams and gave them instruction on what they should do. Since he told us in Acts 2 that in our days we would have dreams, I believe the two I'm going to tell you about were divine interventions in my life.

Tom had just been released from his Air Force commitment, and we had moved back home to St. Charles, Missouri. We had purchased a small house for our family of four and were delighted to begin a new chapter in our lives. Tom was beginning his commercial airline career, and I was delighted to be a stay at home mom of two little ones.

One night I awoke sobbing from a dream that I had in which daughters, Kim and Kelly, were killed in an auto accident. The dream was so real that I remember lying in bed crying for a while. Then I got on my knees and prayed for protection over them. I asked the Lord to send his angels to guards us. "For he will command his angels concerning you to guard you in all your ways." Psalm 91:11

The next day I was driving with the girls taking them to dance lessons. It was raining rather heavily, and I had forgotten about my dream. The girls were both in the back seat of our old station wagon. Forty years ago, they didn't have seat belts, so they were just sitting unbuckled in the back seat. I slowed to brake for a red stoplight at a four-way interchange on Highway 94 South ahead of us. We were first in line to turn left onto the highway when I saw this young girl come speeding toward us. She had attempted to steer right at the intersection but was going too fast for the wet conditions. Her car slid on the wet pavement and came crashing into us. She spun our car around, and I started screaming.

Suddenly the dream returned to my memory. When we came to a stop, I jumped out, opened the back door and was screaming, "Are you okay, are you okay?" to our girls. They were both crying, flung to the floor of the car. I reached in, got them out and checked them over. They seemed a little dazed but okay. I was shaking but thanking God for sending His angels to protect our daughters.

The front end of our old station wagon was bashed in, and the car was totaled. I didn't really care. Kim and Kelly were bruised but okay. I was so grateful I was warned to plead His angels' protection that everything else paled in comparison to His Goodness to us. "The angel of the Lord encamps around those who fear him, and he delivers them." Psalm 34:7

The other powerful dream I recall happened in Montana before we moved home. I had pleaded with Tom to go to a prayer meeting and concert at our church. He went even though it wasn't his first choice on how to spend that evening.

That night I had a vivid dream. We were in heaven, and he and I were truly united in faith in soul and spirit. I remember waking up and feeling so peaceful. I rolled over and looked at Tom. He was awake also. He said, "I just had a dream that we were walking together in heaven." I was totally amazed. He described the same dream as mine.

This was so encouraging to me, and I pondered it a lot when our marriage was in jeopardy three years later. It reassured me that we were to be partners and help each other on this earthly journey toward our heavenly destination. Sometimes we don't understand the "whys" of divine dreams; but when we know they are heaven sent, we need to ponder them as Mary did. We can learn from Mary's example as she trusted God in every situation. "But Mary treasured up all these things and pondered them in her heart." Luke 2:19

God-IN-cidence #9 Never Give Up

"A longing fulfilled is sweet to the soul."

Proverbs 13:19

I cannot read this proverb without thinking of the long struggle my good friend Ann had conceiving her fourth child. She desperately wanted another baby and spent over two years trying different methods and hormones along with doctors to help them. She consulted fertility specialists and went through extensive tests, drugs and even laser surgery for endometriosis. Still no conception occurred.

Finally, the doctor told her she had less than a two percent chance of conceiving if she didn't use fertility treatments which she refused to do. She began this quest so hopeful that the Lord would answer her prayer; but after months of crying every month when she realized another possibility passed, she got very discouraged. Her desire was so very strong and persistent that I also thought surely this must be God's will for her. He says, "Take delight in the Lord and He will give you the desires of your heart." Psalm 37:4

During this time, I prayed and beseeched the Lord to give this dear friend a child. She had stood with me and prayed earnestly many years before that my marriage would be restored, which it was. Now I was standing in the breach for her. Even with all the grim medical consultations she relayed to me, I still prayed for her heart's desire.

One day I felt led to write a poem concerning all this. This was truly an unusual thing for me to do. I never write poetry; I solve math equations. I wrote it on a stiff golden yellow piece of paper and had even cut three butterfly shapes down the left side. The words just welled up inside me and spilled out on paper. Ann had become consumed with having a child, and the rest of her world lost its focus including the "joy in the Lord." To understand the poem which is another God-IN-cidence that I wrote it, I need for you to know more about Ann.

Ann is a wonderful, creative, spontaneous person. When she gets an idea, she runs whole-heartedly with it. With each new venture she attempts, she works diligently at it. No halfway job for her. It will be as near to perfect as she can make it. She will plan, re-invent, change, revise and plan again.

Once when we lived a few miles apart, she decided to open a Christian dance studio. Although she had never run a business before and had no experience or background in dancing, she didn't hesitate a minute. She rented a couple spaces in a strip mall and hired some Christian women who were dance instructors. After a couple months, she had quite a lot of clientele. It was so endearing watching three to sixteen-year olds dancing to songs praising the Lord. She even had lessons for the mothers who wanted to be taught some new dance techniques.

Our two girls took lessons there and danced in the recital. It was a wonderful production performed at the local high school's auditorium. The music, costumes and dances were first class. Her whole venture was successful and doing well, but then her husband got transferred. Although her dance studio didn't last very long, I was amazed how she conceived a dream, planned and worked so hard until it was accomplished. It was a great undertaking, and I'm sure the Lord smiled upon it.

When the reality of a move sunk in, she switched gears and began to pray for a beautiful house in the country instead of another one in the suburbs. I was sitting in her kitchen, agreeing in prayer with her, and she asked God for country acreage, horses, and a bay window in her kitchen so she could watch her horses. Now mind you, she had never had horses before. I was astounded she knew exactly what she wanted and was bold enough to petition God for everything.

I will never forget the first time I visited her in Louisiana. I walked into a beautiful house in the country with a huge bay window in the kitchen. Of course, running right before my eyes were newly purchased horses. Now Ann didn't buy an old, slow trudging horse —no, of course not. She bought a beautiful young spunky red mare for herself and an older gelding for the kids. They enjoyed those horses for years.

As I said, she amazed me with her ability to plunge headfirst into new ventures. She was always busy creating or working at some project. She appeared to handle and accomplish everything she set her mind on.

Then the issue of another child arose. This was an area where sheer grit or determination wasn't the deciding factor. It was whether it was God's sovereign will to bless them with another child. After hearing her so upset on the phone month after month and then year after year, I spent a lot of time interceding on her behalf. Yet, getting weary of waiting myself, I began to wonder if maybe she wasn't supposed to conceive another child.

Then after prayer one day, the words of a poem poured out of me. It just flowed. I wrote as fast as they came to me. Then I put it in an envelope and mailed it off to her explaining it was the first poem I ever remembered writing after a time in prayer.

At the top of the paper it said:

Ann

March 1991

Butterflies are free

And Ann again you must be

Up above your worries and cares

Flit and fly where no one else dares

You did it before with Christian Dance

You soared with a dream—

Failure? NO CHANCE

That desire in your heart

Budded "praise in dance" to start

Though some said, "Don't be a fool"

Ann looked to the Lord—

Not caring to be cool.

And now new dreams have taken root

A baby with a new house in the country to boot

"Negative, negative," say signs all around,

But my dear Ann's temper will soon abound.

She'll blast those ole demons

With one shout of faith,

And soar like a butterfly

Beautiful and safe.

Love in Christ

Pat

She called and said she loved it. More months followed with nothing happening. Then, she said, one day while she was riding her horse, she finally relinquished HER will. She told God that if He didn't want to give her another child, to please change her strong desire for one to His desires for her. She quit all the charting, pills, etc. she was doing. She finally seemed at peace though disappointed.

Over the next couple months, her phone calls revealed an acceptance of the situation. I also had accepted the possibility that a fourth child was not in God's plan for her. This happened in May 1992.

That August I flew with my daughter Kelly to Virginia for a visit with Ann at another new location. They had been transferred and moved again. I remember getting into her car in the airport parking lot.

Now, as I look back on it, the events move in slow motion. I see her look at me as I get in her car with a big grin on her face. Then I see her hand with a yellow piece of paper moving towards me. She keeps smiling and staring at me. I look at her dumbfounded since she hasn't spoken a word. She then starts waving the paper back and forth saying, "Pat, Pat, don't you remember the poem you wrote?" I was still speechless, not comprehending what she was implying. Finally, Kelly piped up from the back seat and said, "Mom, she is going to have a baby!"

I screamed, shouted and we hugged for joy. After years of hearing her cry and then after her confession of final relinquishment of her will, I had let go of it also from my mind and prayers. I was thinking I was going down to see their new location, not celebrate a new baby on the way. It was such a joyous moment that only two close friends, so bound together as we were, could really relish.

Justin was born the next March, beautiful and healthy. He was such a delight to them as their other three children were older and soon on their own after his arrival. Last year, in 2018, we went to North Caroline to his wedding. All these memories of his birth flooded my mind as I watched Ann get teary during the mother/son dance at the reception. God knew during all the years of her weeping that she'd be dancing with him at his wedding.

We all come to places in our lives where we must surrender our will to the Father's. Sometimes He says yes and sometimes He says no. We need to trust that He knows what is best for us. Ann had to lay down her desire. Her surrender brought victory. Just like Abraham had to trust when God told him to sacrifice his only son Isaac on the altar after He had also been told he would be the father of many nations. (Genesis 17:4) Could Abraham understand that? I can't imagine how he could, but he trusted God and surrendered his desires and will to Yahweh's. "As the heavens are higher than the earth, so are my ways higher than your ways and my thoughts than your thoughts." Isaiah 55:9

Ann is a very accomplished artist. She teaches all over North Carolina and has won awards for her beautiful watercolors. All her paintings reveal God's glory in nature. She graciously let me share one of them with you in this book. If you would like to see more of her work or order some prints, go to http://www. annieglacken.com.

God-IN-cidence #10 Diamonds from Heaven

"I lift up my eyes to the mountain

Where does my help come from?

My help comes from the Lord

The Maker of heaven and earth."

Psalm 121:1-2

Life was busy in our household. I was balancing teaching high school mathematics with raising the last two of our five children. Active in our church and my school, I didn't think my schedule could handle anything else. My husband Tom was an airline captain, so we squeezed in family time when he was home between trips.

However, life was about to become much more complicated after I went in for my yearly mammogram. I was totally blindsided when the doctor told me I had stage 3 breast cancer. I was almost as shocked as I was the year before when I looked at my wrist and my diamond tennis bracelet that I'd worn for twenty years was suddenly missing. The anniversary gift I never took off was nowhere to be found.

Now I felt like another huge loss. Control? Peace of mind? My health? I couldn't even name the conflicting emotions riveting me.

After the lumpectomy, my doctor discovered it had also spread to six lymph nodes. I kept thinking that this isn't supposed to happen to someone like me. There was no history of cancer in my family.

I wanted to continue working during the treatments. My co-workers took over my classes the week after each chemo treatment because I was too weak. Family, friends and the teachers showered me with food, gifts and encouragement. My dear husband took over the cooking, household duties and transporting the boys when he was home. All the support was wonderful, but it still was a bleak time in my life.

Our oldest daughter Kim and her husband were due to deliver their second child during the middle of my chemo treatments. I really wanted to be present for this exciting event. They also needed help caring for their two-year old son, Peyton, during Kim's hospital stay. So, I asked my oncologist if I could travel to Denver from our home in St. Charles to help her. Since her scheduled C-section was two weeks after a chemo treatment, he thought I'd be strong enough to go. I was elated.

The nurse who administered my chemo told me that the week I planned to be in Denver was the very week my hair would begin to fall out. She suggested I take a wig with me. I don't know if it was more a case of denial or logistics on how to pack a wig with a Styrofoam base, but I didn't take it. I did grab a few stretchy turbans and threw them in a roomy old straw handbag---just in case.

It was such a joyous moment when they wheeled little Emmett Patrick in his basket out to the waiting room so I could see him. He was perfect and beautiful in every way. I was so thankful that I could be there. I lingered, staring at him, but then it was time for me to get back to their house to watch little Peyton.

When I got back to their house, I noticed a few strands of hair had begun to fall out. On my, the nurse was right! Daddy Jason was spending the day with Kim and baby, so I had to wait until the next day to do something about it. I played with Peyton and tried to ignore my shedding.

The next day, I went to the hospital to visit Kim and baby Emmett. When I went into the hospital's lobby, I noticed that vendors were selling purses to raise money for a charity. I spotted a bright red handbag. On impulse I decided to buy it. Naturally, I wanted to help the vendors and their cause. I also needed something bright and cheery because my hair had started falling out in clumps that morning, and I felt sad. I usually buy dark, traditional types of purses, but that day I decided to break out of my mode. I didn't like the big, worn straw purse I had brought along with me. In fact, I hadn't used it for a long time and had debated throwing it away. I only took it on the trip because it was big, roomy and good for traveling.

Later in the day when I returned to my daughter's house, my hair continued to fall out. In fact, as I was snuggling with little Peyton on the couch, some hair fell out on him. I decided then and there I had to do something. They couldn't bring a newborn home to a house covered with my hair. So, when Jason got home from the hospital, I went to a local salon and asked the stylist to cut my hair to one-half inch all over. I just couldn't muster the courage to tell her to shave my head. I really didn't want to be bald. I loved fixing my hair, wearing make-up and being feminine. This was hard for me. I left feeling dejected with a turban covering up my sprouts.

My spirits had been good prior to this because I believed with God's intervention, I would survive. I chose to listen to inspiring songs, read Scripture and only dwelt on positive messages. I truly believed the Scripture, "And we know that in all things God works for the good of those who love him, who have been called according to his purpose." (Romans 8:28) I didn't have any idea what good it would do me, but I trusted that He did. Yet, losing my hair had made me feel vulnerable and sad. I was missing my husband and feeling lonely.

Daddy Jason had gone to see the new baby again, and Peyton was asleep besides me on the couch. I said a prayer for help and then got an idea to switch purses. Having something pretty and new will cheer me up, I thought. I began to empty my belongings from my old straw purse. When I thought the old purse was empty, I picked it up to discard but heard some jingling.

What could that be? I then noticed the lining in the purse was ripped near the top. So, I turned it upside down and gave it a shake. Out came a few coins but also the two broken strands of my lost diamond tennis bracelet!

Tears flooded my face. I was so overwhelmed with the timing of God's touch. I couldn't believe my eyes! I never thought I'd have a string of diamonds like that again. Since we hadn't taken out a jewelry insurance rider, I couldn't replace the lost bracelet. I had resigned myself that my bracelet was lost and gone forever. Now the realization struck me that God was safe keeping it for just the right time. I felt bathed in His love.

The gold links connecting the diamonds were very worn. One must have broken when I had reached in my purse or got caught in the lining's rip and broke. The broken bracelet pieces evidently slipped behind the lining of the purse to be hidden at the bottom of it. Of all days to find it! No way was this a random coincidence!

The excitement of finding the bracelet assured me of God's loving care, and the anxiety of walking through the rest of my treatments was greatly diminished. I knew He was with me and watching over me. I even spoke at my school's assembly and told the entire student body this story of God's blessing to me.

Since the links were worn, I had the diamonds removed from the bracelet. I decided to share them with our two daughters. I divided them in thirds. Kelly and I had ours made into diamond crosses, and Kim put hers in a dinner ring setting. It gave me joy to see my surprise gift multiplied. The picture below was taken when we wore our new diamond creations on Christmas 2007.

One April day in 2007 will never be forgotten; the day I looked up and saw strands of diamonds falling to me from Above.

My parents with me on Mother's Day 2007

(A condensed version of this story was published in *Angels on Earth* magazine in March/April 2018.)

God-IN-cidence #11 A Series of Mini-Miracles

"Now to Him who is able to do immeasurably more

Than all we ask or imagine, according His power

That is at work within us, to Him be glory in the church

And in Christ Jesus throughout

All generations, forever and ever. Amen"

Ephesians 3:20

It began after a tragedy in our family. My brother's wife of twenty-five years died from a complication following a blood transfusion to cure her leukemia. She was in her early forties and left him and their teenage son and daughter. They married at eighteen, high school sweethearts. They had some rocky times in their marriage but carved out a successful construction business in the boot hills of Missouri near Branson. They had worked hard, long days and weekends to establish a business that was known as one of the best in the area. After Geri was laid to rest, my brother Tom went back to his business and immersed himself in it.

Soon, we heard stories of a big buying spree he was on; new trucks for the business, a computer system, and a motor home. He was usually conservative, and this seemed out of character. I was wondering if he was covering up his grief and loneliness with a barrage of 'toys'. We all do that at times.

Then a realtor convinced him to buy acres of hilly, undeveloped land near Branson for millions of dollars. She said the Missouri Highway Department was going to put a major highway right through that property and someday he'd be a multi-millionaire building gas stations and developments along the way. He was so excited about it, but my family and I were concerned. It was a huge loan for him to take on. Yet, is business flourished, and he managed fine with his two children and their spouses working with him.

He met a wonderful woman named Anna. He fell in love with her and so did our whole family. She loved to have fun, cook, bake and be a mother to his children and hers. Anna and Tom were so happy living on the lake, working and enjoying their children and grandchildren.

Then the recession of 2007 hit. That land mortgage became a noose around his neck growing tighter each year. MODOT, the Missouri Highway Department, eventually put a highway through his property but granted no access to his property. He fought it with lawyers to no avail. He tried to sell it, but no one was developing property or buying large tracts of southern Missouri land at that time. He was stretched to his limit. It got to the point that he couldn't continue to use all the profits from his construction business to pay the land mortgage and still run his business.

My family and I had been hearing these frustrating stories about this land dilemma for years at every family gathering. We had been storming heaven for an answer. None of us, including our parents, had the kind of money to help him ward off the bank's threats to bankrupt him personally and his business. If he went under, his entire family would lose their livelihood.

"God, please have mercy" was our cry. Tom looked as if he was at a breaking point during one period. My family just kept praying and telling him to hold on. Then one Mother's Day weekend, he and Anna drove to St. Louis to see our mother at a family gathering. After hearing again, the newest part of the saga about the bank taking everything he had worked 35 years for, I was inflamed.

The bank had already repossessed the land so those 10+ years of payments were lost to him, but they still wanted to bankrupt him and bleed his business dry. They wouldn't re-finance the remaining balance again and lower his payments. He said he was going to court soon, and his future would be determined. I blurted out, "I wish I could talk to that judge and tell him what a hard-working, honest businessman you are. It's the state of the economy right now that neither you nor the bank can sell that land. Lots of homeowners and businesses are getting special financing or allowances at this time because of the severe recession." I was just venting.

The next month I went to a Rotary sponsored youth leadership camp called RYLA to work as a counselor. I loved working with the teenagers and seeing their enthusiasm. One of the area's Rotarian men came to welcome the kids and give a little speech.

Soon after, it was time for lunch. I was talking with my group of campers, arriving late to the cafeteria. All the seats at the adult counselor's table were taken, so I went up front to occupy an empty seat. A few minutes later, the speaker and his wife came and sat directly across from me. We exchanged greetings and began our meal.

Current topics came up and soon we were discussing the St. Louis Cardinals. The speaker said, "I saw the pitching coach for the Cardinals last week, and he looks like he lost a lot of weight compared to his TV image." I then piped up and said, "That's probably because his wife is dying of cancer. It's sad. I know that because he is my brother's neighbor and good friend. In fact, he built his house."

The speaker looked directly at me and said my brother's name! I said, "Yes, that's my brother, the builder." When he said that, I assumed he had heard of his great reputation for building quality, custom homes in southern Missouri.

The next words out of his mouth took my breath away. He said, "I am the mediating judge between the bank and him in his land case."

Time stood still. My heart was beating out of my chest. It was as if all the noise of the loud kids in that cafeteria was silenced. I just saw his eyes staring at me.

And then I began to talk and talk and talk. I told him my brother's whole life story. I told him of his honesty and faithfulness of making the payments until he absolutely couldn't. I told him about his efforts to sell it with no success. I told him about the bleak future of his children and their families if the business was stripped of its assets and equipment. I told him how the bank had received his monthly payment for over 10+

years and now had possession of the land to sell when the market was better. Then I asked what more could he do if no one would buy it, his business was slow, and he had already re-mortgaged his house against the land?

I must have been so passionate because the judge's wife came around the rectangular table next to me and said, "May I give you a hug?" I said, "Of course." Then the judge said, "I think it will be okay." He stood, said good-bye and left.

I walked outside of the building, went to a private place and wept. I mean, I sobbed and sobbed. All those years of prayers, waiting, hoping and believing culminated in a luncheon sitting across from the judge of his case. I was completely astounded.

How many little miracles convened to make the judge and me volunteer our time at that conference the same week? Then to sit across from each other in the large college cafeteria, have a casual conversation about the Cardinals, and then he mentions seeing the Cardinal's coach, my brother's neighbor, the week before. Also, his remembering my brother's name and being assigned as the judge on his case were such incredible happenings.

My brother's house and his business were spared. He made a cash settlement with the bank, and they did not press for liquidation of his business assets and equipment.

Tom's family and business are flourishing. Restoration miracles-- what a faithful God we serve.

God-IN-cidence #12 Carolyn's Children

"He fulfills the desires of those who fear him;

He hears their cry and saves them."

Psalm 145:19

I had written "baby for Carolyn 10-12-2000" next to the above Scripture in my bible. I have a habit of writing people's names, prayer requests or answers to prayers next to the Scriptures I pray for the individual circumstance. I was praying for her and entered that date when she was so fearful she would never conceive. She had many fertility problems and had to have an operation to remove one ovary. Then she couldn't get pregnant even after all of that. Frustration was building as she was taking temperatures, charting changes and hoping against hope every month she would have good news.

We used to meet for lunch when any of us sisters celebrated a birthday. We were meeting in the first week of August for our sister Deb's birthday. Carolyn had just suffered a miscarriage days before. She bravely tried to put a happy front on that day, but her pain was evident. Prayers and more prayers ......that's all we could do.

What a happy day it was for me when I wrote "PTL Kieran 6-13-2001" next to the above verse when her beautiful baby boy arrived! It happened to be 9 months after the first time I wrote the date next to the plea for his birth. God is so good.

After Kieran's first birthday, Carolyn and Keith started talking about their hope for a sibling for him. Carolyn started out optimistic but then battled waves of fear that another struggle might be in store.

On October 11, 2002, my daughter Kim, Carolyn and I met for dinner in Chesterfield, Mo. before going to a two-day women's retreat. Carolyn was very somber all through dinner and then finally said her period had started which was very upsetting. She said she was afraid she'd be a lousy roommate with us and maybe she should just drive home. Kim and I wouldn't hear of it and insisted she stay for the retreat and overnight with us. She reluctantly agreed.

At the retreat that evening, the most amazing thing happened. Carolyn walked up for individual prayer after a time of singing and worshipping God. When she sat back down at our table, it was soon time for a break before the next talk. The lady, a stranger, sitting next to Carolyn said to someone else at the table, "I want to name my child Kendall if I have a girl." Carolyn perked up and said, "That's the name my husband and I picked out for a girl, too!" Since it was such an unusual name, I was amazed. Then I heard a little whisper in my heart that she would soon conceive and get a daughter to name Kendall. I told her that, and she smiled and hugged me. Lo and behold, she must have conceived very soon after the retreat because Kendall Virginia Conboy was born July 9, 2003.

"And I will ask the Father, and he will give you another advocate to help you and be with you forever—the Spirit of truth. The world cannot accept him, because it neither sees him nor knows him. But you know him, for he lives with you and will be in you." John 14:16-18

As Kendall was approaching two years, Carolyn expressed her desire for another child. But she said, "Pat, I don't know if it would be better to have a sister for Kendall or a brother for Kieran?" I said, "Let's pray and let God decide." So again, we went to the Father and asked Him to bless them with another child.

I still remember exactly where I was standing in my kitchen when the phone rang with her voice screaming into the phone, "MY LIFE IS OVER, MY LIFE IS OVER, MY LIFE IS OVER..." I almost panicked thinking something horrible happened. Finally, after asking what happened, she said, "Triplets!"

She had been so happy to find out she was pregnant the month before but never dreamed of multiple births. I guess God solved her dilemma of whether to have a brother for Kieran or a sister for Kendall. Ha! Their lifestyle was over as they had known it.

When the triplets arrived, everything revved up to super speed in that house. He gave Kendall two sisters to play with and Kieran a baby brother. She carried them 35 weeks which is marvelous for a mother with triplets. They were also great weights of 5 lbs. 5 oz and two of 5 lbs. 6 oz. Mother and babies were all home within 6 days of deliveries! They didn't have weeks of neo-natal trips and all that added stress. God made these deliveries and this part of their family journey easier than most. The babies were so beautiful and so different with red, black, and brownish/blond hair colors.

Now that they are thirteen years old, Maeve, Rory, and Liam are as unique and different as their hair color. Carolyn, my baby sister, is a happy mother with her quiver of children.

"Children are a heritage from the Lord, offspring a reward from him. Like arrows in the hands of a warrior are children born in one's youth. Blessed is the man whose quiver is full of them." Psalm 127:3-5

God-IN-cidence #13 My Life-Long Dream

"May He give you the desire of your heart

And may all your plans succeed."

Proverbs 20:4

I always wanted to go to Israel and walk the land Jesus did. Yes, we believe by faith and not by sight, but I thought it would be wonderful to see the places of His miracles. I never had a specific plan on when I would get there, but the desire was always in my heart.

A friend of mine, Denise, asked if I wanted to go "treasure hunting" with her one day. I said, "Of course." We hunt bargains or treasures among the four to five re-sell-it stores in our area. We find trinkets for our grandchildren or must-haves for us. Sometimes nothing pops out at us, but we still have fun.

As she was pulling into my driveway to drop me home, she commented, more to herself than me, that she couldn't forget to send her money in that day for her pilgrimage to Israel. I piped up and said that I wanted to go. She then explained all the details, and I was so excited to find a friend who would relish the trip as much as I would. I saved my teaching money that year to pay for the trip as I considered it my upcoming birthday present to myself. Tom was working and couldn't take off. Besides, summer was not the season he wanted to be over there anyway. It's very hot then.

As we were approaching departure, my 91-year-old Dad went into hospice because of heart failure. His doctor said he could have weeks, months or even a year. That made my decision more difficult. Neither of us had paid an extra $300 for cancellation insurance for the trip, and I was beginning to feel uneasy about leaving the country with him in that condition. I prayed and still didn't have any peace, so I felt I should just ask him. He said, "Go, of course you must go." So, I did.

Then Denise contracted a severe case of viral pneumonia right before the trip. I called some friends from home and asked them to pray for her. She forced herself to pack and fly to Denver to visit her daughter as planned a couple days before our overseas flight from there. When she landed in Denver, she was so ill, her daughter took her immediately to the hospital where she was admitted. We were both dumbfounded because we thought for sure God would heal her because we asked so many people to pray.

My friend Rita called that day and asked how Denise was doing since she was one of my friends praying for her. I told her she couldn't go; she was in the hospital. I then said I felt so sad because I really thought Denise would recover. I then wondered if I could have someone else use her trip since she couldn't get a refund anyway. I mentioned that to Rita, and she said she'd love to go. I thought, why not? This happened two days before the trip began.

When I called the tour agent, he said there was no way she could use her plane ticket and go in Denise's place. I then asked if she could use the land package because the bus seat and double bed hotel rooms were available. He said he would check on it but doubted it could be arranged in time. I called Rita with the news, and we prayed that if it be God's will, He would bless her with this trip. The agent called the next day saying yes, she could have the land package FREE.

The next day when I called Rita, she was so excited and said you know it's my birthday today. I had forgotten. I think God gave her a $4000 birthday present! She bought a plane ticket and met us in Tel Aviv. This was such a blessing for her because she was still grieving over losing her husband. He died of a heart attack just five months prior. I was so grateful to Denise for giving her the land portion and that I had a traveling companion.

Sailing on the Sea of Galilee and prayer-walking the Via Dolorosa I consider two highlights of my life. Words can't really describe what transpired within me during those ten days, but I will treasure it always.

Why didn't God answer our prayers and heal Denise? We don't know. But Denise's daughter had a terrible accident and broke her femur ight after Denise had left the hospital to recover at her daughter's house. I'm sure she was glad her mother was there with her because she was in excruciating pain. Would Denise have been able to enjoy Israel concerned about her daughter? As it worked out, they both helped each other recover while we were across the ocean.

I thought I would be the one to cancel the trip. After a few days home in Florida to rest, I flew to Missouri to be with Dad. The timing was perfect because I was with him a few days before he left this earth; only 10 days after I returned from the pilgrimage.

He told my niece the day I arrived, "Live a life praising God." I never heard words such as that out of his mouth, but he "lived" that saying every day. When I commented to my brother what an unexpected response that was, he said he verbalized what he could no longer live. I had never thought of that it that way.

None of us know why the events occurred as they did, but we do know the trip was an extraordinary blessing for Rita and me. I also believe God has a special gift to come for Denise. No one could convince Rita that her ten days in Israel was a coincidence. No, we know, it was another GOD-IN-cidence.

At Qumran, site of the Dead Sea Scrolls

God-IN-cidence #14 My Dad's Eulogy

"Then I heard a voice from heaven say, "Write: Blessed are the dead who die in the Lord from now on." "Yes", says the Spirit, "they will rest from their labor, for their deeds will follow them."

Revelation 14:13

Dad's funeral service was a collaboration of ideas from Mom and each of us six children. We spent a couple days discussing how to best honor him and pick the songs and readings he would like. Each of his seventeen grandchildren participated someway, and each of the seventeen great-grandchildren walked up and put a carnation on his casket. At some of our relative's funerals, each of the deceased's children spoke a few words. We all thought that was so touching.

I had assumed we would do something similar, or if not, I would speak because I was the oldest child. I think I was half in shock after he passed because things had been happening so fast. I recently returned from my Israel pilgrimage and then soon was in a house of mourning. I was still exhausted and fell into a deep sleep each night.

The second night after Dad passed, I woke up at 3 a.m. and felt a compelling urge to write about his life. I didn't have a pen or any paper, so I sneaked around in the dark because I didn't want to wake my mother. The words just poured out of me and I scribbled them down as fast as I could.

The next day we were sitting around Mom's dining room table talking about who was going to speak. One brother and one sister didn't want to do it. I really wanted to, but I did not voice that because then I thought all of them might feel pressure to participate. It was decided only one brother and one of my sisters would speak. I had previously felt the Spirit must have woken me up to write in the middle of the night, but then I thought it was to put into words what my Dad meant to me.

On the morning of the funeral, my sister texted me and said she wasn't going to speak because her speech just wouldn't come together. I grabbed what I had written earlier, threw it in my purse with no time to reread or revise. I trusted it was what I was supposed to say.

"Man, fully alive reveals God's glory." That prophecy seems to sum up my Dad's life, I think. Dad totally focused on the people, situation or job before him at the time. Because of this focus, he enjoyed working while he worked, and he worked hard; enjoyed family when it was family time; enjoyed church and its functions when he was present there; enjoyed volunteering for church committees and working the yearly church picnic in the sandwich stand. He made 36 four-day silent retreats and brought other men along to be blessed. He LIVED the moment! How WONDERFUL is that!

One special area he loved being present in was time with Mom. God says in Proverbs 5:18 to "delight in the wife of your youth." This was probably the easiest of God's commands for him to do. He loved everything about Mom. He gratefully blessed and ate every delicious meal she put before him. He played cards, rummikub, slots at the casino, or whatever she wanted him to enjoy with her. He worked along side her designing and building frames for the boat covers she sewed. They did everything together and loved it that way.

One of the best memories I have of him was watching his face when Mom would casually go from conversation into one of her jokes. I loved watching him try to refrain from smiling so he wouldn't give away that a joke was coming. Close to the punch line though, his bottom lip would begin to quiver, and then I knew a joke was on its way. Sure enough, he and all listening would soon erupt in smiles and laughter.

When the flood of 1993 washed away his crops and destroyed his home, he just pressed on. He took on life's challenges as they were dealt to him, keeping on in the only way he knew to live: loving God, Mom, his family, and all his many friends and neighbors.

Even now as we wait weeks to lay his body to rest because of the high flood waters covering the road to the Portage des Sioux cemetery, I'm sure he's smiling and saying, "Patience Pat."

What a GIFT it was to be his child.

Coincidence or God-IN-cidence that I woke at 3 a.m. and wrote hat eulogy?

God-IN-cidence #15 Small Sweet Happenings

"Whether you turn to the right or to the left, your ears will hear a voice behind you, saying, "This is the way, walk in it."

Isaiah 30:21

About a month ago, when Tom and I were reading the Sunday paper, I was in the Lifestyle section when I noticed an article about a remodel of a living room that was basically the same layout as ours. I showed it to Tom, and he said he really liked the arrangement. We instantly got up and began rearranging our furniture. We had to move one chair out of the room, but otherwise our place had the same furniture arrangement as the paper's.

What was unusual is that we were having crown molding installed in the house later that week like the model in the newspaper. Since we changed our living room around, we made different choices in the molding. By the end of the week, our entire open living /dining room looked totally transformed. What was also great about it, is that we loved it.

Tom said a couple days later, "I really like our new living room changes, and I don't think it was a coincidence that you noticed that article, that we both agreed on the changes, and we did it right before the installation of the molding and the re-painting.". No, not a coincidence at all. Thank you, God.

A week later, I was browsing in a boutique back in our hometown of St. Charles, Missouri. It was located below our apartment complex. Since I was the only customer and I had time to spare before my nail appointment next door, I made small talk with sales attendant. I told her how we live in Florida but go back and forth to Missouri a lot because of so many family members. She wondered how we ended up in Florida. I told her we visited some friends who live in a subdivision called Whitmore but vacation the month of February in Florida. I asked if she

new where Whitmore was, and she said yes because she lives next to it
n Windcastle. I said, "Where do you live in Windcastle?" and she
answered with our old house number. I excitedly said, "That's the house
we custom built." We both looked at each other and said, "I don't
believe this!"

She was as happy to meet me as I was her. We discussed some
of the unique features we designed in the house. It was fun seeing her
and getting to hear that they enjoy the house and pool as much as we
did.

Speaking of that custom house we designed, the timing of its
closing was perfect. We sold and signed the papers to relinquish the
prior home the day BEFORE we closed on our custom-built home. It had
been on the market for 18 months. Believe me, we were earnestly
praying for it to sell because two house payments would have stretched
us to the limit. God rescued us again.

The next day I went to our granddaughter's first birthday party. I
told our son about running into the lady who bought our old house. He
said, "That's wild, how does that happen?" I smiled.

Another sweet memory was during Tom's furloughed time and we
had no money coming in at all. I hadn't gotten my teaching job yet. I had
been going to a prayer meeting at church and during prayer request time
that week, I asked for prayer to meet our bills. I didn't elaborate because

we had recently moved back to Missouri and I was new to the group. A few days later, the doorbell rang, and this sweet lady named Shirley walked in carrying bags of groceries. I was surprised and when I thanked her, a tear rolled down my cheek. I was touched because of her kindness but even more so that it was my birthday which she didn't know. I realized WHO did.

Five days ago, our neighbor asked us to come over for an impromptu 5 p.m. get together. A bunch of neighbors were happily talking away when I arrived. I sat next to someone I didn't know, and she proceeded to tell me that she was a good friend of the hostess and not a neighbor.

We chatted, and she told me she loved to cook but her spare refrigerator in the garage had just broken. I then said that I had one to sell. I gave her a bargain basement price, and she was thrilled. We had ordered a bigger refrigerator that was to be delivered the next week. Our new one was delivered yesterday, and our new acquaintances were there to haul off the existing one.

She said how remarkable it was that we sat next to each other at the party and that she would end up getting my refrigerator. No, not remarkable, just my final God-IN-cidence for this book.

Epilogue

Your Creator is trying to get your attention and touch your life. So many people are wandering around this earth thinking there's no plan, no guidance, no reason other than to survive and find a little pleasure along the way. I'm hoping that by sharing these stories, your eyes will be opened to look for God taps in your life. They have made me so aware that a Divine Presence intervenes in my daily life. You DO have God-IN-cidences also. Acts 10:34-35 says "God is no respecter of persons", which means He shows no partiality. Our Creator wants to commune with you also.

Think about it—why did He make us with intellects and free wills? That free will has caused wars, devastation and horrible evils. He could have made humans like the animals that perform as designed. Then we could have acted in a predicable way taking care of ourselves, others, and this planet we share. Animals act on instinct, not free will. He didn't want more animals; He wanted intimate friends in which to have a relationship. We can't force people to be our friends. It's their choice just as it our choice to accept God's friendship.

So many people have a false, misrepresented image of God formed by ignorant teaching or extreme hurts in life. They don't know God is a Loving Father, always giving good gifts to his kids. So why do bad things happen? Too big of a topic to cover in this book, but it involves demons, free will, and life lessons learned only by suffering.

We have a choice in this modern age to look and seek Him or be distracted by a techno world. Being bombarded with noise, it is hard to escape to hear His still, small voice. Facebook, Twitter, internet, cell phones, headsets, video games, computer programs.....the list goes on and on. In the past 60 years, the bombardment of our serenity began as TVs filled every home and people moved from the outside to inside for relaxation and entertainment.

When the Industrial Age hit America, farmers and ranchers gave up their peaceful, meditative way of life for the noise and clanging of factories. Soon wrap around front porches disappeared from new houses and back decks were constructed. Instead of watching sunsets or talking to family and neighbors, everyone hibernated in front of the box. Then, when video and cable came on the scene, more and more entertainment was put at our disposal. It almost becomes hypnotic to collapse in an easy chair and flip channels. Now add to all this social media, and our time is totally occupied.

To prove this point, I've gone with our daughter's family to build 400 square feet homes for the poorest of poor in Mexico. The house compares to a small garage in the states. With a lot of volunteers, this small dwelling is constructed in four days with only electricity provided for the occupants. There is no heating, air-conditioning, or inside plumbing. The new residents are thrilled and most cry with gratitude! They had been existing in make-shift hovels before.

A year after my first trip, we went back to build another house. We also wanted to visit the family we built the home for the year before. We walked in, and, much to our amazement, smack dab in the center room was a T.V.

To understand our surprise, you need to know that their water is delivered weekly and stored in open barrels in front of the house. They cook and bathe from dipping out water from those barrels. Flies and bugs also rest on the top of the water. They endure the heat in the summer and the cold in the winter. It's hard for us to imagine an existence like that, yet they scrape up enough money to somehow purchase a TV. So, from rich to poor, everyone is being flooded with information and noise.

Now all of us are getting attached to our cell phones. The iPhone and iPad are truly prophetic named symbols of this I-generation. It seems to me our country is so divided, and too many people are only thinking of "I-wants." We feel lost without being able to instantly communicate with each other. Thus, constant interruptions are being added to the constant noises. No wonder people feel overwhelmed and agitated.

Were we designed to have all this stimulation? I taught high school kids for 33 years, and the steady increase in ADD, ADHD and behavioral issues was astounding. Could it be we are overloading our nervous system? Do toddlers run and explore as we did, or are they propped in front of videos to entertain them and make them quiet? How is their creative energy stimulated if they watch flashing colors and hear noise constantly in their homes or day cares? How will they learn to wait to hear the small, quiet voice of the Father? Young or small, is anyone still, attentive or listening?

Some may think that God should shout louder than anyone else to get our attention like a political pundit does on TV. He doesn't operate that way. One story from the bible tells us how God speaks to us.

A prophet named Elijah went out to meet God. "And behold, the Lord passed by, and a great and strong wind tore into the mountains and broke the rocks in pieces before the Lord, but the Lord was not in the wind; and after the wind, an earthquake, but The Lord was not in the earthquake; and after the earthquake a fire, but the Lord was not in the fire; and after the fire, A STILL SMALL VOICE." 1 Kings 19-11-12.

Beautiful sunsets shout God's majesty. Even the birds tweet songs to their Creator as colorful dawns burst forth. The intricate details of a flower bud show the handiwork of the Master. Animals roaming this earth in balance with nature reveal a master plan. All creation reveals an order that only a Supreme Being could engineer.

All the various skills and talents of people that operate for everyone's needs to be met is a phenomenon that amazes me. Someone desires to be an undertaker, someone an engineer, someone a teacher, someone a plumber, someone desires and fulfills the services we humans need to function in this world. Yet, sometimes we take this for granted. The ordinary becomes mundane, or as the saying goes, 'Familiarity breeds contempt.' Isaiah 54: 16 says "See, it is I who created the blacksmith who fans the coals into flame and forges a weapon fit for its work."

I know one thing; our Father God loves us and will find a way to get our attention. When I was diagnosed with stage 3 breast cancer, a lot of my priorities shifted. My family was my total focus. My dear friends became even more cherished treasures than before. Teaching my students was still important to me, but I was willing to let go for a season to recover. Clubs and activities came to a halt. I spent every available minute praying and focusing on the people I loved.

It was a season of refocusing and re-evaluating my life. I didn't like that dire circumstances forced me to slow down, but maybe that is what it took for me at that time. It was a time of suffering, introspection and keen alertness. I noticed special moments of blessings in ways I might have glossed over before the diagnosis. God even blessed me with the grand surprise that I shared earlier in this book.

Noting God-In-cidences in our daily routines is certainly a more joyous way to rejoice in our Father's Presence than in suffering. Yet, He loves us and desires such an intimate communion that He will design a personal plan to get our attention. We are the work of His hands. Even if we walk away, He sends out love messages continually. I'm sure He performs every love tap specifically for each unique personality.

Again, I hope relating these will help open your eyes to His workings in your life. He's always there. He's always calling. Are we listening?

If we open God's love letters to us, His Word, and read and meditate, we fill our soul with His presence. So many people deny themselves this gift. The divine treasure collects dust on the shelf instead of working shifts in the heart of man. His Word transforms us into people who can see and recognize His workings. Otherwise, one walks around in a stupor as if blind, plowing through their daily routine, ignoring His road map of directions. Would people throw away love letters from their beloved before their marriage without even reading them? I doubt it. Yet, the Word of God, our Creator's love letters to us, is discarded by many.

Many in this blue-tooth generation will not set foot in a church or synagogue. Some believe they are part of the Christian family because of their heritage, but their hearts are given to the material world. Many professed Christians and Jews alike relish their label, but the unseen

piritual realm has no relevance to them. They pass by a place of worship
n the way to the mall or golf course.

Others say they sense God in nature, and that's enough. So
many people are spiritually emaciated but physically buff. Others are
ntellectually superior but atrophied in wisdom. Others know they are
amished for something substantial and fulfilling but don't know where to
ind the answers.

In this restless age, some people fill their time listening to divisive
political debating or opiniated talk show hosts, binging on shopping
renzies or joining numerous sports or club activities. We can't escape
our environment or the advances in technology but need to strive to
carve out a quiet retreat somewhere and somehow in our daily life.
Everywhere we go, there is someone screaming to get our attention.

A lot of times if I don't set aside my usual morning quiet time, I
feel something amiss all day. Or maybe I've filled my day with so much
activity that I can't seem to quiet my soul to listen to Him. He is the
Hound of Heaven says the poet Francis Thompson. He will track us down
however He wishes. How much better is it if we set aside a block of time
to be still and listen? This is so hard for us Americans. We are used to
talk, activity and more talk with activity. Listening is an art that is
beginning to erode just like cursive handwriting. We are drive-through
food seekers for our soul as well as for our body.

When we recognize God intervening in our daily life, besides the
pure joy that floods us, there is also a profound peace that follows: A
KNOWING, a contentment realizing our Father God desires to touch and
bless us, and the awareness that we are part of His kingdom. These gifts
are sweet tastes of bigger joys to come and a revelation that "our steps
are ordered by the Lord." Psalm 37:23

As mentioned, God doesn't operate as we do. As Deuteronomy
4:29 says, "But if from there you seek the Lord your God, you will find
him if you seek him with all your heart and with all your soul." He's given
us the church. He's given us His workings in creation. He's given us love
letters. And most of all, He's given His precious Son by sending Him to
walk on this earth teaching us about the Father's love and plan for us.

Yet only a few rejoiced and grasped the Gift when He came down to earth, while most rejected Him. Thus, He was slain and crucified for our salvation over 2000 years ago, but nonetheless, even now He woos us. Will we humans constantly run from our own healing and joy? God says to, "Open wide your mouth and I will fill it." Psalm 81:10

He longs to bless you, and I long to bless you as well. Of course, my desire is smaller than a grain of sand compared to His ocean of burning Love for you. I just want all of you to know the joy and sweetness I've found in recognizing the Father's Hand in my life. I have been so excited writing and sharing my stories of blessings with you.

"Even when I am old and gray, do not forsake me, O God, till I declare your power to the next generation." Psalm 71:18

There could be no ending to this book. I hope to receive and recognize God-IN-cidences until I take my final breath on this earth. So, I'm going to stop now. If you'd like to share some of your God-IN-cidences or ask me any questions, please email me at windcastle6@aol.com. This book is available on Amazon.com. as an eBook or paperback. Select *all*, then *select*, then type *Pat Watson*.

May God bless you and may you be watching for His surprises!

All Scripture quotes were taken from the *New International Version or New American Standard Bible*

Discussion Questions

1) Have you ever noticed a God-IN-cidence is your life? If so, explain it and your reaction?

2) Do you believe that God is trying to communicate with us, or are we just on this earth to try to figure things out on our own?

3) What is primary way you hear God's voice? Is it in reading His Word, observing nature, people telling you their experiences, worshipping Him, through preaching, or in God-IN-cidence type happenings?

4) Does it encourage you when people share their stories of how God speaks to them? Why or why not?

FROM THE DESERT TO SUPERSONIC

WHY ME?

Testimonial by Tom Watson

Where it all began:

Forbes Air Force Base, Topeka, Kansas. 1949

Dad was an Air Force pilot and Mom was a home- maker. Dad was adopted because his mother died giving birth to him. His father had five other children and didn't think he could care for a baby. So, my dad was adopted by his fraternal aunt who was married to a Watson. So, I am really a Davidson by birth.

Fast forward. After Dad and Mom's divorce when I was living in Kansas City, I remember the night I met my stepfather. Well, that night in 1953 was the night I was told we were moving to Saudi Arabia; Mom, me at three, and my new stepfather.

Airplanes

That was when I took my first airplane ride and was fascinated. That was it! I was on my way into aviation as a three-year-old.

audi

Loved it. My stepdad worked for Aramco, the company that eveloped all the world's oil. The company is still in operation today. I rew up mainly in Dhahran with short stints in Abqaiq and Ras Tanura. Aramco had a huge compound for us. It was like living on Air Force base. The elementary school in the compound was taught by American teachers. For high school we had to leave Saudi, so most of my buddies and I went to Notre Dame International in Rome, Italy. This was a Catholic American school run by the Brothers of the Holy Cross. What an adventure. I was a B student and loved math. I loved to read National Geographic and read about the space program, anything related to flying or space.

St. Louis, 1967

College was beginning and the school I chose was in St. Louis, Missouri. It was a small aeronautical engineering school named Parks College, which was part of St. Louis University.

The most important part of my life was on September 17th, 1967. and some of my frat brothers went to a small girl's college in St. Charles, Mo. This is the night I stuck my finger out and looked at an awesome lady from Portage des Sioux, Mo. I asked for a dance. She was already going steady with a guy who was in college in another part of the state.

Long story short, Pat and I will have been married for 50 years in 2020. I remember the walk to the chapel at Parks where I asked the Lord to bless me with Pat's presence for the rest of my life. Prayer is powerful and it was the best gift I have ever received.

Pat and I dated. She was in college to be a math teacher. I had joined Air Force ROTC at Parks and graduated as a second lieutenant in the Air Force. During college I had become a private pilot. Pat and I were engaged and in the fall of 1970 we married.

Air Force, 1971

Vietnam was raging and the Air Force needed pilots badly. Pat and I ended up in Big Spring, Texas at Webb Air Force base. I began pilot training scared to death. How could this guy from Saudi Arabia even think he could succeed? Buttttt guess what? I loved it and ended up second in my class and was assigned to be a T-38 instructor at Webb. The T-38 is a supersonic jet that at one time held the world time to climb record. Twenty-three years old and I was instructing in one of the world's premier aircraft. I received numerous awards. Life was good. Pat was my rock. Baby number one was born June 1975. Her name was Kimberly.

Air Force in Montana, 1976

After the wind down of Vietnam, the Air Force needed fewer pilots and many were given their walking papers. I survived the cut; however not as a pilot, but as a Missile Combat Crew Commander in charge of Minuteman III missiles in Montana of all places. We grew to love it. During that time our squadron was being modified, and my work schedule allowed me to work on getting all my civilian flying ratings while hoping for an airline job. Baby number two was born in October 1977. Her name was Kelly.

Airline Career, 1978

Was offered a job with hometown airline Ozark and left the Air Force. Pat was thrilled. She was home again in St Charles, Missouri around her family.

Wasn't too long and I was furloughed in May 1980. I flew odd flying gigs, but the most important thing I did was volunteer for the US Army reserves as a helicopter pilot in the Huey and Black Hawk. Shortly after that, I was recalled to Ozark and began a 33-year career with different airlines. In 1986, TWA bought Ozark and in 2001, American Airlines bought TWA. I flew international for TWA and had many international trips where I was privileged to have my family with me.

During this time, I was still in the reserves. I went to Desert Storm and ended up in Dhahran, Saudi Arabia where much of this life story started. I also was gifted with 3 boys during this period; Kyle, Tommy, and Zach. I retired from the reserves in 1999, loving every minute of it. I was then a MD80 Captain and later advanced to a 767/757 Captain.

Retirement, 2012

Couldn't believe I was 63 and finally quitting the job I love. It was never really a job. My dream in retirement had been to buy a diesel pusher. A bigggg diesel pusher and travel around the country. One day I woke up praying and realized that was not a good investment. We had owned 2 airplanes over the years, and they were mainly money pits and in the shop. This looked like a similar disaster. Cancelled it.

New Adventure, 2013

We arrived in Oxford, Florida at 8 pm on New Year's Eve, 2013. Oxford is on the outskirts of The Villages. We had decided to look at Florida as a possible residence. Pat landed a part-time teaching job in Clermont, Florida so we leased a small house for the month of January 2014. On the way down from Missouri, she says to me, "Let's take this slow and not jump into buying the first house we see." We still had a home in Missouri which we planned to keep and were considering a second house in Florida sometime. Yeah right, I was thinking. Have we ever taken anything slow? Our life has always been supersonic.

Well, it took all of four days and we had a contract on a home in The Villages. That was slow? The Villages is one of the most unique communities in the U.S.; golf cart community with over 50 golf courses. Amazing place.

One year later, we bought a bigger house in The Villages and eventually sold our Missouri home. We moved to an apartment in St Charles, using it as a part time residence, since we established residency in Florida and live there.

70 years old, 2019

Guess what? I am currently working as a flight instructor for Flight Safety International training pilots in corporate jets and Pat is still an adjunct college math professor. Some day we might retire. We now have 7 grandkids and are so blessed with all our successes. We don't take it for granted. Life is good.

Not long ago one of my clients at work told me he was amazed at my life story. I agreed, and I thank God every day for all the blessings I've had over my lifetime. My dreams came true. All of them. Family is most important. My career was a miracle. I have done things that only a few people on this earth have had the opportunity to do, not by my hand, but through God's blessings on me. He was the architect. Supersonic is the only way to describe it.

Never give up...Have a dream...Believe in God...Work hard

Believe in yourself...Love your family

Tom Watson

Made in the USA
Columbia, SC
16 February 2021